£3.95

© 1989 GRANDREAMS LTD

Edited by *Melanie J. Clayden*. Design and layout by *Louise Ivimy*. Written and researched by *John Kercher*. Additional material by *Melanie J. Clayden*. Photographs supplied by *Duncan Raban* (*All Action Photographic*), *Retna Pictures Ltd*, *Scope Features*.

This is an independent publication and has no connection with the television series or the production studios. All information is correct at time of going to press. The publishers cannot be held responsible for any changes that may have occurred in the story lines. We regret we cannot enter into any correspondence regarding the series.

Published by
GRANDREAMS LIMITED
Jadwin House, 205/211 Kentish Town Road,
London NW5 2JU

Printed In Italy

ISBN 0 86227 672 1

CONTENTS

The Show They Couldn't Stop! 6

A Profile on Alan Dale 10

A Profile on Anne Charleston 11

A Profile on Guy Pearce 12

"How my career took off" by Kylie Minogue 14

A Profile on Anne Haddy 18

Neighbours behind the scenes 20

A Profile on Paul Keane 24

By Royal Command 26

The Punk who turned Hunk - Craig McLachan 28

Pin Up 32

The *Neighbours* Quiz 34

A Profile on Vivean Gray 38

A Profile on Annie Jones 40

The Multi-talented boy next door - Jason Donovan 42

Did You Know? 48

What to look forward to in *Neighbours* 52

"My recipe for success" by Stefan Dennis 54

A Profile on Fiona Corke 58

Let's meet Ian Smith, Sasha Close and Lisa Armytage 60

Quiz Answers 61

The show they couldn't **STOP !**

It seems quite incredible that the first showing of *Neighbours* went out on British television screens in the Autumn of 1986.

Nobody, including the programme planners could have imagined that this Australian soap opera about a group of people consisting of just a few neighbouring families, many of whom were young, would take off in the phenomenal way that it did.

What was even more remarkable was that initially it began in what is termed 'a daytime slot'. Soon fans of the show were so great that it was decided to put the series on twice daily, which brought in even larger audiences to the extent that today, the ratings top the twelve million level.

Practically every member of the cast has become a star in his or her own right, often more popular than they are in their native Australia.

And people like Kylie Minogue, who was once earning the standard soap fee down under of something like £250 per week, became a pop star and vaulted herself to the status of millionairess!

Then there have been the off screen dramas too, like the much publicised real life romance between Kylie and Jason, or that between former *Neighbours* stars, Peter O'Brien and Elaine Smith.

The entire cast invaded Britain for the Royal Variety Show and stayed on to appear in pantomime.

It seems strange then, that when the series was first launched it was decided by the original Australian television network which took it on, to axe it after just 170 episodes.

But no-one had expected there would be such an uproar at the decision to shelve the show. Fans began to write in until it had a snowball effect. By this time a rival television network, picking up on what was happening, decided to take on the show, inject some money into it, and launch a publicity

campaign and put the series back on the air.

Huge promotional events were arranged which created havoc in many cities as tens of thousands of *Neighbours* fans clamoured to see their favourite stars. And suddenly, the soap had become one of the most popular in Australia's television history.

Ramsay Street's real location is 'Pine Oak Court' in South Vermont, where the cul-de-sac houses value at $100,000 each. The real life residents are sometimes inconvenienced by a few of the over the top fans. Plants and even mail boxes have been ripped from the ground. The situation was such that now a watchman patrols the street at night.

But just what makes the show such a success? especially with young people. Stefan Dennis who plays Paul Robinson says: "I think it's down to a few reasons! A lot of the cast are young, but on top of that there is not anything out of the ordinary. It's very true to real family life which a lot of soaps aren't. Nothing is so expensive as to make it fantasy like the *Dynastys* of this world.

"Mostly it's about real people in real situations and the problems the teenagers have in the series, are the types of problems that teenagers around the world can relate to!"

Despite the fact that many members of the cast made off from the series to do other things, it hasn't in any way dampened fans enthusiasm for the show. New characters appear who in turn have built their own fan following, and it looks like nothing.can stop the popularity of the show that was once destined for the bin!

A PROFILE ON

Alan Dale

JIM

Alan Dale who plays Jim, the head of the Robinson household, has a tough job keeping his authority over the younger members of the family.. However, he usually handles things in a diplomatic fashion and comes through on good terms with everyone.

Like so many of the cast, Alan's origins don't lie in Australia at all, he grew up in New Zealand.

"I was about thirty when I first went to Australia to look for acting work," he says.

But he had plenty of experience because since he was a kid his parents had run an amateur theatrical group and he had enjoyed playing in many different productions. "It was a lot of fun," he says. "I bet a lot of youngsters would love to have the chance of doing that."

When he isn't filming, Alan enjoys getting out and into the water, as so many Australians do.

A PROFILE ON

Anne Charleston

MADGE

Anne Charleston says that she is amazed at the amount of mail she is sent due to her role as Madge.

"It really is incredible how so many people want to write and find out everything they can about the series and me as a person. But it's encouraging."

However, away from the *Neighbours* set, Anne tries to unwind by getting away from it all and doing ordinary things.

"I like to go to restaurants and the theatre. Despite the fact that I'm an actress I still get excited about a new play that is being put on," she says. "It might seem like a busman's holiday, but I never see it like that because my work is a pleasure. And I can thank my mother for that. For it was she who sent me to drama classes when I was young. I didn't fancy the idea but once I was there you couldn't drag me away!"

A PROFILE ON

Guy Pearce

MIKE

I f Guy Pearce, who plays Mike Young, ever wanted an alternative way to make a living, then he knows it would be music.

"There's nothing I like better than getting together with other musicians, and having a good session," he says. "In fact I wouldn't mind forming a band some day and making records."

He plays saxophone and piano and has plenty of talent and ability.

He has taken time off *Neighbours* to play John Dysart, a 60's Aussie rock star in *Heaven Tonight*. 'Jeopardy' one of Guy's compositions features in it and is released in Australia. But at the moment he is enjoying himself acting with the cast of *Neighbours.*

He broke into acting from a determination created at school.

A sports freak, he was well into bodybuilding and all ways of keeping himself fit. Nobody was more pleased than he when he landed the role in the series.

His fan mail is enormous and he confesses that he does get mobbed by girl fans.

When he relaxes at his home it is usually by writing music, composing songs for the day when he gets that group together!

14

How my career took off

KYLIE MINOGUE

When Kylie Minogue walked into the studios to audition for the role of Charlene Mitchell, way back in the beginning of *Neighbours,* neither she, nor anyone connected with the series could have imagined the enormous success that she was going to have.

In fact, her original contract was for just one week! That seems laughable now when you consider the superstar status that she has achieved!

Whilst everyone in the series is popular with fans, it is Kylie who has managed to hold the attention. And not just the fellas. Possibly more girls than boys write in their thousands to her every week.

Kylie was actually born and bred in Melbourne where Ramsay Street is set. "I've lots of friends here," she says, "but the real problem these days is trying to find the time to be able to see any of them. I know that they must sometimes think I'm being offish when I say that I'm too busy, but that's the truth. Since the series and the recording took off I don't even have time to spend with my own family. And that can be a bit of a hassle because I really like being at home.

"I suppose it's just one of those things when your career suddenly takes off the way mine has done. And it was all so unexpected. The Minogue family are fairly close

anielle who is 17, and brother
endan, 18.
Although her mother used to be a
allerina, there was really no
owbusiness influence put on Kylie.
fact it was Danielle who got the
cting breaks first when their
other took them along to audition
r a television role.
But it was Kylie, after landing a
art in *Skyways* and a few other
ows who took the lead. She
onfesses that she doesn't have a
t in common with her screen
haracter of Charlene. "I suppose
s only natural that people who
atch the programme assume that
e're the same, we're not!"
Kylie has an uncomplicated home
e and gets on great with
veryone. Even fans of the show
no meet her are pleasantly
rprised at how approachable she

Even without the hit records, Kylie
as a cover girl on dozens of
agazines. She had been voted
ost popular personality in Australia
nd won several awards for her
cting.
Now she is adding gold and
atinum record discs to those and
on might even need a special
om just to house them!
Kylie admits that her greatest wish
ould be to run riot in the shops.
ve never gone mad and bought
ally expensive stuff before," she
ys. "But I'm probably the world's
eatest browser. It's just the fun of
e whole thing."
Even at school she always looked
ward to Saturday when she
ould meet up with her friends and
end all day going around the
pres. Now she is able to do that
an International scale and would
obably go back home with
nkloads of new clothes if she

didn't put a bit of restraint on
herself.
But she says that she doesn't want
to go in for a flash lifestyle. "You've
got to keep your feet on the
ground," she says. "And just
because someone is a huge
success now doesn't mean you are
still going to be at some point in the
future. So I save."
However, she has splashed out on
a place of her own which is more of
an investment than a desire to
escape from home. "I'm always
back with the family whenever
possible," she says.
What every *Neighbours* fan really
wants to know, however, is whether
Kylie does intend on marrying her
co star, Jason Donovan.
Kylie just smiles politely and provides
the usual 'just good friends' answer.
Apparently they've known each
other since they were kids
appearing in *Skyways*. But they also
spend a lot of time apart, since
Kylie is travelling so much and Jason
also has many of his own projects to
attend to. They might have made
plans for the future for when they
have both established themselves,
but it's probably far too soon to
signal wedding bells!

6

What Kylie likes most of all, is to be able to escape from the pressures once in a while. She is so intent on being in touch with her fans that this often prevents her from taking chances of the leisure time. But when she can, she likes to be able to just hop on a bicycle and drift off into the wide open spaces.

She also says that she is not one for too much clubbing or anything like that. "I'm on the move so much with all the flying from country to country, the recording and personal appearances, that I just like to put my feet up and have a good natter on the telephone," she says.

Now, however, Kylie, is becoming a name to reckon with in America. Her records have been doing well in the charts there after phenomenal success in Europe and Australia. She might just have to start doing promotional and television work there too!

Despite the fact that she has had number one singles and albums, Kylie insists that she won't give up acting. "I would like to be able to balance the two careers. Other people have done it and I think that it is possible."

However, she must watch that she doesn't exhaust herself too much. People often worry about her looking frail but she says that she feels fit, and that it's nothing that a really good night's sleep won't put right!

She could never have imagined just how prophetic her single 'I Should Be So Lucky' was going to be for her. It looks as if she is going to be around for quite a long time. But, we might just see her taking a few more holidays. Anyone who can keep up her kind of working schedules and not want a break would have to be superhuman!

A PROFILE ON

nne Haddy

HELEN

From the age of twelve Anne Haddy, who plays Helen Daniels, was adamant that she was going to be an actress. She was an only child who went to Adelaide High School. "The art teacher there was Keith Michell, now the actor. In a school play *Androcles And The Lion* he did my make-up. Years later I met him backstage after one of his plays in Australia, he didn't want to know when I told him he used to teach me art!"

When Anne left school she took to radio plays, as television hadn't started in Australia. "I went to England when I was twenty three in the hope of finding acting work, but I ended up working for Kellog's."

Anne's career has included plays at Sydney Theatres as well as 70's TV work, including presenting a *Playschool* programme similar to ours.

Anne admits that she is not rich despite parts in *Skippy, Prisoner Cell Block H, Sons and Daughters* and *The Young Doctors!* "The work in Australia is regular rather than rich. I don't think I've taken a day off from *Neighbours* since I took the part of Helen. I think that lorry drivers get more money than soap stars, I wouldn't mind a bit of Joan Collins' money!"

Neighbours
Behind the scenes

Working on *Neighbours*, as with many soap style series', might look like easy work, but you have to be as tough as they come to stand the enormous pressures of the job.

Elaine Smith says: "When most people are still in bed we have to be at the studio ready to be made up for the day's filming. That means getting up at maybe 5 o'clock in the morning, which is no joke in the middle of winter!"

Trying to get into your character whilst most people are sitting down to breakfast in the comfort of their home is also difficult. But then this is what

Behind the scenes

soap operas are all about. They are about pressure to complete what has to be done every day. There is not the kind of luxury that you get on a major film where it is possible to push certain things into the next day.

There aren't the lavish budgets either, so filming has to be done to a tight schedule. *Neighbours* is being shown five days every week and that means five different scripts to learn every week too for the actors and actresses.

"It does mean that your social life can be hit quite a bit," says Jason Donovan. "You get home at night after maybe eleven or more hours at the studio and then you have to sit down and start rehearsing your lines for the next day's filming."

So if you think they go out dancing and socializing afterwards then you can forget it.

They usually just want to go to bed and get a good night's rest. It's only at the weekends that they get a chance to unwind!

And even then there is often work to do. The cast of *Neighbours* are so popular that they are often invited to do promotional events like opening shops or appearing in department stores, not to mention all the other media demanding things like radio and television.

But they are paid quite well for these; often many more times the money that they receive for their work on *Neighbours*. So at least they get

something from it.

It does, however, make them feel quite exhausted on occasions. Stefan Dennis says: "I often have to fly hundreds of miles at a weekend to make an appearance somewhere or the other. It does wreck whatever plans you might have for relaxation, but then you just have to think to yourself that this is part of the job and you are being paid well for it!"

Of course, in the summer, the cast find it pleasant when they have to do outside location shooting. They might find themselves on the beach occasionally, which is a nice break from the hot studio lights. The studio itself, in Melbourne, is where all of the interior sets are built for the houses of Ramsay Street.

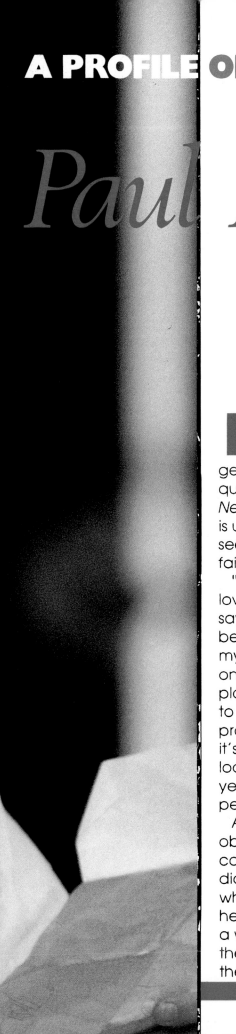

A PROFILE ON

Paul Keane

DES

Paul Keane, who plays Des Clarke, is generally dubbed 'the quiet one' on the *Neighbours* set, which is unusual because he seems to have lived a fairly exciting life.

"One of my great loves is music," he says. "I like nothing better than getting out my drum kit, putting on some records and playing along. I try to get in as much practise as I can, but it's not as easy as it looks. It can take years to be a real perfectionist!"

Acting wasn't an obvious choice of career for him. "I didn't quite know what I wanted to do," he says. "I drifted for a while before I hit on the idea of going on the stage."

Since then he has been in constant demand, and with *Neighbours* he has found a bunch of real friends. He might laugh at the 'quiet one' tag, but says that he does like to spend moments away from everyone and everything.

He loves sports and reading and says he is amazed at the amount of fan mail that he receives.

The *Neighbours* cast during rehearsals for the Royal Variety Show. They performed in front of a delighted audience, which included British Royalty. After the show they were presented to the Queen Mother and Princess Margaret.

CRAIG McLACHLAN

ALIAS HENRY

The wonderful thing about *Neighbours* is that they seem to be able to produce good looking young men like a magician produces rabbits out of a hat. No sooner does one hunky star leave the series, another one arrives to build his own fan following.

Craig McLachlan is the one who, as Henry Mitchell, filled the gap left by the departure of Peter O'Brien who played Charlene's cousin, Shane. Craig has now built an enormous fan following with sackloads of mail arriving at the studios every day for him from his admirers begging for autographs and photographs.

But whilst Peter O'Brien might have been dismayed at the thought of being a pin up and talked of as a sex symbol, Craig would appear to be more in tune with these things. He openly admits: "Ever since I was a kid the whole star thing appealed to me but then I wasn't certain whether would make myself famous in music or as an actor! Now realise that it's possible to be at the top in both of these professions if you can balance things properly." Recently, however, Craig has had those well loved locks of golden hair cut because, "I wanted to have a more mature look which was a bit different from when I had a mane." But it doesn't seem to have made any difference to his appeal. If anything it might just have increased his fan following. He admits that when he first took

on the role of Henry, Charlene's brother, he was quite nervous. "People can say all they like about soap television being a piece of cake, but that's far from the truth.

"We all have to work extremely hard for twelve hours a day or more, and everyone is completely professional. But what scared me was the thought of going into such an established series and trying to be accepted by both the cast and the fans of the show. It's not an easy thing going to *Neighbours* for your first day."

Craig needn't have worried because it only took a few episodes for him to be drawn into the whole excitement of the show and realise, from the letters he began to receive, that he was as much loved as everyone else. "Everyone gets on so well, I couldn't believe it," he says. "And when you have to work with the same people every day for such a long time, it's just as well."

Craig, however, might be in the super hunk mould but he is the first to confess that things weren't always like that. "When I was a kid, I was really thin," he says. "So much so that the other kids at school even used to tease me about it, That was when I decided that I ought to do something about my physique."

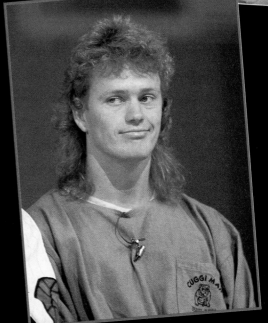

He became a regular at a gymnasium doing weight training and strenuous exercising. In no time at all he had emerged a superman with shoulders that looked as if they could hold a jeep on them.

Craig's character of Henry, however, counteracts the beefy image by being a bit mischievous and good for a laugh. It is this which parallels a side of Craig's own lifestyle.

"I hate taking things too seriously. You can become so involved in work that you forget to laugh. So I do enjoy playing the odd practical joke now and then to liven things up a bit. But then I was always like that when I was a kid, and some of the stunts I used to pull frequently got me into trouble."

When he moved to Sydney he took on work in TV commercials, but his first break was when he took a role in *The Young Doctors*, although he had been wanting to be an actor long before that.

"I suppose I really came into my own when I starred in a musical production that was put on at my

lifestyle. It was quite frightening."

So off he went back home and ended up doing all kinds of strange jobs. "One of them was working as a plumber's mate and I had to clean out toilets," he says. "Needless to say, I didn't stay doing that for too long."

But what Craig did do was take up his love of singing. "It was something I'd also done when I was at school," he says. "I was the kind of fella who would approach a group playing in a club and ask if I could do a few numbers with them. And a lot of them agreed."

He used this talent to join another band, which he describes as being a punk group, although he confesses that he was not a punk himself. "To be honest I found the audiences at the concerts we did quite frightening." So he got out of the scene.

Then *Neighbours* was offered to him. But there was a slight problem in that he hadn't watched any of the series. "You couldn't get away from people talking about the programme, but I couldn't relate to it because I was always busy working and never got back in time to see it."

Craig did some quick catching up and soon found he was accepted for the role of Henry. It is rather coincidental that it is Kylie, who plays his sister, who has soared off to music stardom, when Craig himself still nurtures an ambition to make records.

"People might think that this is just another actor who wants to be a singer, but that's not true," he says. "Music is a great part of my life and I would love to be able to act and establish a recording career too!"

So watch out, those charts could soon be seeing his name alongside that of Kylie and Jason.

school," he says. "Because I was a bit of an extrovert, I suppose it came across and I was lucky to be seen by someone in the business who offered me the chance to do it professionally."

But once in acting he was dismayed at the way that his life would change. "I wasn't used to the big city life," he confesses. "When I came down from the small town I lived in to do *The Young Doctors*, everything was a bit intimidating, like it is for anyone who arrives in a metropolis after a casual

So you think you are a real fan of *Neighbours*? Then put your knowledge to the test by trying to see how many of the correct answers you can come up with in this quiz! Not only do you have to know the show well, but also the backgrounds to the stars in it.
Good luck!

1. Which former *Neighbours* star had to overcome his fear of flying when he took on a new role as a pilot in a different television series?

2. Can you name the star who in his private life used to be nicknamed 'Dunnybrush'?

3. Before Scott married Charlene he had a stag night party. What were his friends and relatives going to dress him up in for a practical joke?

4. Anne Haddy once played a Fat Lady in a musical. Is this true or false?

QUIZ

8. Which *Neighbours* star is married to a former Miss Australia?

9. What is Kylie's sister's name?

5. What was the reason given as to where Henry Mitchell had been when he first appeared in *Neighbours*?

10. What year did *Neighbours* start being shown in Britain?

6. Who, whilst he was at school starred in *I Can Jump Puddles* and *Skyways*?

11. Elaine Smith starred in a pantomime in England with Peter O'Brien at Christmas 1988. What was the pantomime?

7. Who do you think almost knocked out Jason Donovan in a rehearsal scene on the *Neighbours* set?

12. What is the name of the television company which produces *Neighbours*?

35

13. Who nearly got to play rugby for Australia?

14. Who won a photographic model contest when she was a teenager?

15. What was the song that Kylie and Jason sang together on stage at a major concert in Australia? It later became a huge hit for Kylie as a solo artist.

16. How did Mrs Mangle come to lose her memory?

17. What is the name of Mike Young's dog?

18. Was Charlene early or late for her church wedding?

19. Who is the father of Daphne's baby?

20. Before he came to live in Ramsay Street where had Des been living? Just the name of the city.

21. How many different videos were shown in Britain for Kylie's first hit, 'I Should Be So Lucky'?

22. Who are the famous record producers who gave Kylie her record success?

23. Scott Robinson put forward Mike Young for a job which he did whilst continuing with his studying. What was the job?

24. The character of Lucy has been played by two actresses. Who are they?

25. Gail Robinson is played by Fiona Corke, who as a hobby plays a certain instrument. What do you think it is; a flute, saxophone, trumpet or a guitar?

26. Paul Keane plays Des Clarke, but which other actor in *Neighbours* also auditioned for the role before being offered his present part?

27. What happened to Des' first wife?

31. When did Kylie appear on screen wearing a completely white face pack?

32. Who plays the role of Beverly Marshall?

33. Vivean Gray, who plays Mrs Mangel, once had a job you would never dream of associating with her. What do you think it was; a dustman, a circus performer, an assistant matron in a boys' school or a store detective?

28. Madge is the elder sister of which character who left the series?

29. Which character did Geoffrey Paine play?

34. Which *Neighbours* actor played the role of Dr.John Forrest in *The Young Doctors*?

30. Charlene Fenn was also in the series. Who was she?

35. Which *Neighbours* star once appeared with a band called *The Y Fronts*?

36. Who was Scott's best man at his wedding to Charlene?

37. Who rescued Charlene from the caravan fire?

38. Which actor in *Neighbours* sometimes writes scripts for the series?

39. *Neighbours* is shot in the suburbs of which Australian city?

40. What does Kylie's brother do for a living?

Answers on page 61

A PROFILE ON

Vivean Gray

MRS MANGLE

Every good soap opera has a mischievous gossip and *Neighbours* is no exception. Mrs Mangel has almost gained a cult following despite the fact that her character is usually quite humourless. It seems that most of her fans can't wait to see what she gets up to next!

But there have been problems for Vivean who plays her role perhaps just a little too realistically for some of the show's viewers! "Sometimes it's difficult to take the insults I get in the street," she says. "People automatically think I am like Mrs Mangel which I'm not. I get some nasty letters too, but I just have to try and tell myself that I must be playing her convincingly to attract this kind of response."

Vivean is not a born Australian. In fact she grew up for the first twenty years of her life in England which might come as a surprise to some of her fans.

She eventually went to Australia and took up acting quite late. "I did lots of jobs before that including working in a shop and as an assistant to a photographer," she says. "But I love acting the best."

Neighbours has made her internationally famous, and in her holidays she likes to travel as far afield as possible, being somewhat of an adventuress.

A PROFILE ON

Annie Jones

JANE

Annie Jones who plays Jane Harris, comes from Hungarian parentage and naturally speaks the language fluently. She started life as Annika Jasko in 1967 and was born in Australia.

The character she plays leads a complicated romantic life as more than one of the *Neighbours* fellas fancies her.

"But it's been a fun role to play," she says. "Just to be in the series for so long has been exciting."

Her entry into acting came by accident when she won a contest in a girls' magazine to be on their cover and it provided her with the idea of doing modelling.

But Annie never had thought of acting. "I didn't do the school plays or study drama."

But it was her modelling which brought her to the attention of the film producers. Her debut was in a film called *Run Chrissie Run* which was screened in the UK in 1985. Under her own steam she began to land parts in various television series including *Sons and Daughters,* which seems to have been the proving ground for a lot of Australian actors and actresses.

Annie has a love of fishing, which might surprise a few fellas who would never dream of finding a girl who loves their sport.

She also likes going to the cinema and confesses that one of her favourite actors is the American actor comedian, Steve Martin!

The multi-talented boy next door

JASON DONOVAN

Make no mistake about it, Jason Donovan is a really multi-talented guy. He's an actor, singer, artist, surfer and, as everyone knows, rides a mean skateboard.

The truth is that, sport apart, he could have made a full time career of any of the other creative gifts that he possesses and, at various stages in his life there must have been some conflict as to just what he was going to eventually make his living at.

He says: "I always loved art, painting and sketching when I was at school. I used to spend a lot of my spare time painting pictures, and my room was full of the various things that I'd done.

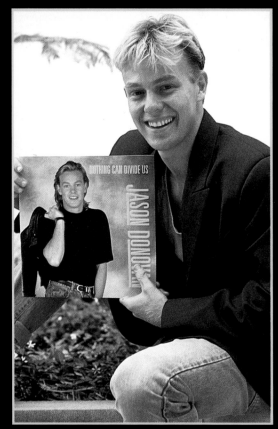

"There was a period earlier on when I considered the idea of making a living from art. Not just locking myself away somewhere like a recluse, but using it in a commercial sense, like for an advertising company or something like that."

For Jason was brought up in a creative environment. His father, Terry, established himself as a major acting talent in Australia, whilst his mother was also well known in television. His mother, however, divorced his father when Jason was quite young and he admits that he hardly ever sees her at all these days. He admits

that it's sad and you sense that there is a certain puzzlement as to why she didn't want to keep in contact with him after she left.

"I grew up with my father after that," he says, "and, because we were both constantly in each other's company, we naturally became extremely close, and I respected almost everything that my father told me." The relationship between father and son was based on trust, and today Jason admits that his father is probably the best friend he has.

"I know that I can always turn to him for advice and that he'll be perfectly truthful and honest with me. He knows what he is talking about when it comes to acting and so I respect that. It's easy to be in the acting profession when you're young and think you know it all. I would never think like that."

Jason probably grew up quicker than a lot of kids of his age simply because of his home situation. Also because he was in the position of being able to go with his father when he was working in television studios or on stage.

"It was a bewildering world at first," he says, "but fascinating and exciting. I thought then that it must be marvellous to be an actor."

He obviously inherited a lot of his father's acting talents. While he was at school he began doing some projects on television, amongst which were, *I Can Jump Puddles* and *Skyways*. *Skyways* was interesting for the fact that a certain young actress called Kylie Minogue also appeared in it.

The fact that Jason was surrounded so much by actors and visits to studios when he was young means that he is free of the flashy lifestyle and ideas that you might expect. In America, for instance,

sons of famous actors would be classed in the Hollywood brat mould.

In Australia, however, things are different, and Jason is a prime example of the guy who just wants to be as normal as possible. "Even now I make certain that I don't lose contact with a lot of my old friends from before I started in *Neighbours*," he says. "They're important to help you keep your feet on the ground."

But despite his father being a famous actor, he advised Jason not to take the risks involved. "He said that it was a really precarious way to make a living and that just because you had one success didn't mean that the situation would continue like that. I knew he was telling the truth but I just had to give it a try! There wasn't any arguing between us, just gentle persuasion and advice which I didn't give in to."

Jason's father is really pleased with him and was the first to congratulate him on his success in the series.

The success of Jason's character,

but always something that a fan can relate to.

"People are writing in all the time saying how things like this or that happened to them and they know just how Scott feels," Jason says.

On ITV in April Jason starred as a 17 year old navel officer in *Heroes*. It was a true life World War Two adventure mini-series. "It's totally different to *Neighbours*, it's very serious, that's why I chose it."

Despite the long working hours on the film set, Jason does manage to continue with his hobbies. He still likes to paint whenever he gets a free moment, and surfing is a great passion of his. "I like to just stick the board on my car and get down to where there's some really good surf to ride," he says.

But if he is in a less energetic and more thoughtful phase, then he finds his relaxation through writing. Yes, he doesn't just sing, but composes and writes lyrics for his material too. March saw the release of his first LP recorded with Stock Aitken and Waterman, after the massive success of 'Nothing Can Divide Us'. "*U2* are one of my favourite groups," he says. "I've got a lot of their records."

A real source of pride for him, however, is the house which he bought. He admits that he didn't like the idea of leaving home, but it seemed right that he should have his own place. "However, I'm round my father's place all the time," he says.

What Jason really likes about his home is that because it required a lot of work it meant that he could design everything just the way he wanted.

Acting might be precarious, but Jason's diverse talents should see him around for a long time to come!

Scott Robinson, in *Neighbours*, is mainly due to the fact that he is so realistic. The confrontation with his screen father, played by Alan Dale, when he announced that he wanted to marry Charlene, would have brought nods of approval from thousands of young people in his position. His father said 'no' because they were too young and Scott still had studying to do, but Scott was adamant that he would go through with it. Eventually, everything was resolved and all were best pals again.

If it wasn't marriage then it might be something equally traumatic,

1. Peter O'Brien, who played Shane, used to be a surfing instructor, before a full time actor. When he went to America, among his pupils were the children of singer, Diana Ross.

2. Stefan Dennis originally went along to the auditions for the series thinking that he was going to be given the role of Shane. But landed Paul Robinson instead!

3. Kylie Minogue and *Flying Doctors* star, Rebecca Gibney, look so alike that when they are together, people often think that they are sisters.

4. Geoffrey Paine, who played the role of Dr. Clive Gibbons loves clothes from the 1950's and has quite a large collection of them at his home.

5. Alan Dale, who plays Jim Robinson, once had to earn a living from delivering milk.

6. Mrs Mangel would hardly seem the type of person who was into jazz, but in real life actress Vivean Gray is a great fan of the music and confesses that she once wanted to be a jazz pianist in a band!

7. Elaine Smith, better known as the late Daphne Clarke is Scottish.

8. Alan Dale once said that he had the pleasure of meeting Prince Charles. Not as neighbours though!

9. Hunky Craig McLachlan as Henry looks as if he could bend iron bars with ease, but he once listed, in an Australian magazine, among hobbies, knitting tea cosies. Now can you believe that?

10. Fiona Corke who plays Gail has an ambition to appear in films and has claimed her dream would be to work with the eccentric comedian, Steve Martin.

11.   Real houses are used in Neighbours and not just sets as in many soaps.   Perhaps the only comparison is the real mini estate of Brookside.

12.   Despite their huge success, Neighbours stars only earn a fraction of what American soap stars do! Hence most of them have bought properties for renovation rather than luxury homes.

13.   Kylie loves huge dangling earrings!

14.   *Neighbours* must be a contender for the record books as being the only series on British television to notch up more than eight million viewers for its weekday lunchtime slot!

15.   Kylie once worked as a shop assistant!

16. While Anne Haddy (Helen Daniels) was playing in the stage play *Bodies* she had a very bad heart attack. "They had to bring me back with electric shock fibrillators, they told me I was lucky to be alive!"

17. Guy Pearce, better known as Mike Young, is actually of English origin. He left England when he was three, but says he would like to return to live here if he left Australia.

18. Craig McLachlan's favourite actress is Minnie Mouse. He says she has "dynamic animal qualities that are so rare!"

19. Anne Haddy is married to actor James Condon, who once starred in *Neighbours* as Douglas Blake.

20. It costs the BBC £5,000 a day for the two screenings of *Neighbours*.

WHAT TO LOOK FORWARD TO IN

NEIGHBOURS

While Britain lags behind Australia by 18 months in the *Neighbours* saga, here's a few of the storyline secrets for you to look forward to.

* Two new villains are introduced played by Julian Branagan and Greg Fleet. These two characters, Ted Reagan and Dave Summers forced Daphne and Gail from the road, resulting in Daphne's death.

* Des Clarke is left to bring up baby Jamie on his own. But not for long! While he is out shopping, Jamie is kidnapped and then abandoned. It is new girl, Bronwyn, played by Rachel Friend, who finds him and returns him safely to Des. So impressed is Des that she is employed as a 'nanny' for Jamie.

* However, Bronwyn is not the perfect angel all the time. She plays a vital role in the break up of Jane and Mike!

* The marriage relationship between Scott and Charlene is none too smooth either, after Charlene finds Scott in the arms of Jane. However, Charlene and Scott are reconciled and decide to give the marriage a new chance. They take a second honeymoon in Queensland, but now it is Charlene's turn to stray. She has a brief affair with driving teacher, Steve Fisher, played by Michael Pope.

* When the two, somewhat distanced now, return home, Charlene finds that she has inherited a house in Brisbane, after the death of her grandfather. So by December, we will have seen her tearful farewell from the series. Kylie says on quitting *Neighbours*, "It was a long and hard decision, but there is a chance for me to return if I want." Scott remains with a job, but the opportunity is left open for him to join Charlene in Brisbane.

* The Robinson household has its own difficulties. After Dr Beverly Marshall, played by Lisa Armytage, marries Jim, they fall into financial difficulties after a business partner defrauds him.

"My recipe for success"

STEFAN DENNIS

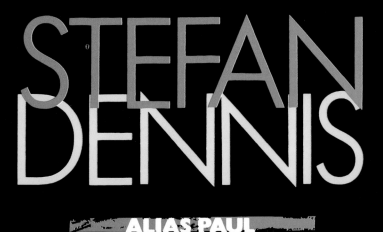

ALIAS PAUL

Anyone who arrived at the home of Stefan Dennis would be in for a couple of surprises, for running around in the huge garden are two goats. And to keep them in check there is also an Old English Shepherd dog.

Stefan, who plays Paul Robinson says: "I have to keep on making certain that the goats aren't chewing up everything they can find. They can be quite active. But I like having them around because it makes me feel as though I'm living on a farm.

"I also have to make certain that they aren't about to butt the cars which are my pride and joy." Cars just happen to be one of Stefan's real passions. "My ambition would be to own a beautiful Porsche," he says, "but I've got to save up a lot of money in my spare time.

"When I do get leisure moments I love to go driving for miles, where you don't see anyone from one hour to the next. My wife, Roz and I are great explorers.

"Soon after we got married we flew all the way to London and bought ourselves one of those vans that you can sleep in. Then we took it across to Europe and travelled to Holland, France, Italy, Germany, Spain and back to London. Then it was the tour of Britain for us.

"It was quite funny, because when we were in London, we used to park the van in a car park near Waterloo Station and we even slept there too. It certainly saved on the hotel bills. But I went back for nostalgia purposes recently to see the place and they've built an office block there!"

If acting hadn't turned out to be his major way of life then he would probably be cooking up some interesting dishes in one of Australia's best restaurants!

"It really came out of necessity that my brother and I did a lot of the cooking at home when our mother was ill. We used to experiment quite a bit in the kitchen and we got quite good at being inventive with meals," he says.

"So after I'd completed my studies at college, I was wanting to be an actor, but I realised that things would possibly be difficult. You really have to chase the acting work in Australia, and so I thought it would be a good idea to perfect a different career so that I would still be able to earn a living between acting jobs."

Stefan went on a chef's course and became qualified and then set out to test his skills. "I worked in dozens of restaurants," he says. "And I always liked to be involved in a bit of fun. I'm a great believer in the fact that cooking should be a good laugh and so I used to mess around a lot. If people weren't into having a few jokes then I often quit the job and went somewhere else.

"But the best time I had of all was when I worked at weekends in a place for old people. All week they were served this stodgy food which they didn't really like. Then I would come in on the Saturday and do all of this cordon bleu cooking. I made French pastries, and the works. They loved it!"

Stefan grew up away from the big city and says: "There was a ski resort quite near to our home and I became interested in the sport and used to go there to practice.

"Even now, whenever I get the

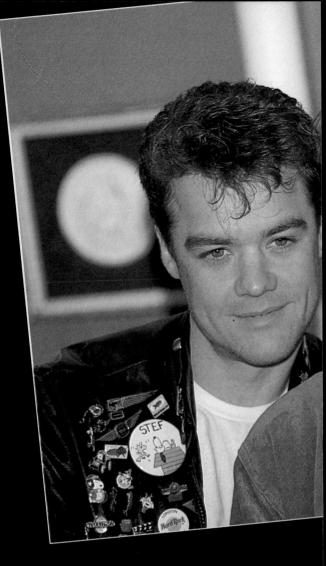

chance I go and ski. It's something I really look forward to.

"I was always into doing daredevil things as a kid. I used to play parachute jumps off my bed at home with my brother. He used to urge me on to make bigger jumps, and one day I did it and broke my leg. That taught me something."

Stefan also had ambitions to be a pop singer. "My brother and I used to put this act together and copy a lot of the records we'd collected. But I don't think that I really wanted to do it more than acting."

However, Stefan did make a record, following on the heels of Kylie and Jason. But he says: "I don't see myself as being a pop singer. The thing is, that you'll probably find that nearly all of the cast of *Neighbours* could sing well

"I lived with my wife in the city for a while, but we felt that when we could buy our own house we would prefer to be further out. So we now live about an hour from the city.

"It's a really interesting house because it was originally owned by a man who was a botanist and he brought some unusual plants from England and other places and put them in the gardens. He also built a lot of small stone walls although the problem was that later owners let the garden get a bit ramshackle. So my wife and I have spent quite a bit of time putting it all back how it should be.

"There are also stained glass windows in the house and we have a large veranda which we can sit out on during the summer." Stefan reckons that he is super active despite the long filming schedules that he does on *Neighbours*.

"I might be working about eleven hours each day," he says, "but when I get home the last thing I feel like doing is putting my feet up. I start working on the house and things like that. I have to keep active."

However, he confesses that it's difficult getting friends to visit him. "They think that an hour's drive from the city is often too far. So we have to go and visit them. But we do have some close friends who'll make the trip here whatever the weather is like."

He also spends a lot of his time flying around Australia doing promotional events. "It certainly keeps me busy, but I enjoy meeting the people. And I still like to travel a lot. I hope that I'll be coming to Britain quite a few times."

And you can be certain that if you were ever invited to his home he could cook you up something interesting.

and make records if they wanted to.

"The situation in Australia is quite different to that in Britain. Because the work is limited you have to be able to do everything from acting to singing to dancing, just so that if something comes up you can take the opportunity. But I don't think you'll find everyone trying to make records!"

The house that Stefan now lives in is one of the rewards of being in such a popular television series.

A PROFILE ON

Fiona Corke

GAIL

Fiona Corke plays Gail Robinson and only through perseverance has become an actress.

"When I used to tell people that I wanted to go on the stage and be on television and films, they used to look at me in a disbelieving way, or as if it was some kind of joke," she says.

Although she later moved to Melbourne, her early life was spent living in the sticks with frequent trips to the city to see her father, after his divorce from her mother.

She later became attracted to amateur theatrical groups, working backstage until she broke into acting proper with small roles at first, and then the break into *Neighbours*.

Fiona says, "I do love travelling. I've already been to America and loved it. I wouldn't mind being able to work there some day in films if I get the chance."

When she finds the time, Fiona loves playing and listening to music.

Let's meet

Ian Smith, Sasha Close
and Lisa Armytage

When Kylie Finkler announced that she was leaving the show, the creators cleverly sent her character, Lucy, youngest member of the Robinson clan, off on a European tour while a replacement was being found.

She turned out to be Sasha Close. At first British viewers' reactions were mixed, but she soon won everyone over and is now fully accepted by one and all.

Before joining the cast of *Neighbours*, Sasha played amongst other parts, a geisha girl in a production of *Madame Butterfly*.

LUCY

HAROLD

Ian Smith, who plays warm hearted Harold Bishop, has seen life on both sides of the camera.

For as well as television appearances in well known Australian series' like *The Sullivans* and *Cop Shop*, Ian also worked as Associate Producer on *Prisoner* prior to taking the role of Harold in *Neighbours*.

The character of Dr. Beverly Marshall is a comparative newcomer to the series. She first appeared in episode 526 but has quickly established herself as a firm favourite with viewers, and her on/off relationship with Jim Robinson is an intriguing storyline.

Beverly Marshall is played by the attractive Lisa Armytage. Lisa is London trained and her acting experience covers everything from television and theatre, to films and even a stint in BBC Radio Drama.

BEVERLY

From page 34

QUIZ
ANSWERS

1. Peter O'Brien
2. Craig McLachlan
3. A chicken
4. True
5. He had been in prison
6. Jason Donovan
7. Kylie Minogue
8. Alan Dale
9. Danielle
10. 1986
11. *Mother Goose*
12. Grundy
13. Paul Keane
14. Annie Jones
15. 'The Locomotion'
16. She fell off a ladder helping Daphne decorate her room.
17. Bouncer
18. Late
19. Des Clarke
20. Perth
21. Two
22. Stock, Aitken and Waterman
23. Working in the coffee shop
24. Kylie Finkler and Sasha Close
25. Saxaphone
26. Stefan Dennis
27. She died
28. Max Mitchell
29. Clive Gibbons
30. Nikki Dennison, Helen Daniels' niece
31. Before her wedding
32. Lisa Armytage
33. An assistant matron in a boys school
34. Alan Dale
35. Craig McLachlan
36. Mike Young
37. Scott
38. Ian Smith
39. Melbourne
40. He is a cameraman